muffins

AND OTHER MORNING BAKES

muffins

and other morning bakes

Linda Collister

with photography by Philip Webb

BARNES & NOBLE

NEW YORK

Text © Linda Collister 2000, 2003, 2006
Design and photographs © Ryland Peters & Small
2000, 2003, 2006

This 2006 edition published by Barnes & Noble
Publishing Inc. by arrangement with Ryland Peters
& Small Inc.

Senior Designer	**Ashley Western**
Editor	**Maddalena Bastianelli**
Food Stylist	**Linda Collister**
Stylist	**Mary Norden**
Production	**Patricia Harrington**
Art Director	**Gabriella Le Grazie**
Publishing Director	**Alison Starling**

2006 Barnes & Noble publishing

ISBN-13: 978-0-7607-8284-2
ISBN-10: 0-7607-8284-9

Library of Congress Cataloging-in-Publication Data

Collister, Linda.
  Muffins and other morning bakes / Linda Collister ;
with photography by Philip Webb.
      p. cm.
Rev. ed. of: Morning bakes. c2002.
Includes index.
  1. Muffins. 2. Baking. 3. Breakfasts. I. Collister, Linda.
Morning bakes. II. Title.
  TX770.M83 C65 2003
  641.8'15--dc21
                                    2002154361

Printed in China

1 3 5 7 9 10 8 6 4 2

Notes: Before baking, weigh or measure all ingredients
exactly and prepare baking pans or trays. Weighing scales
and a set of cup measures are recommended for use with
these recipes. Ovens should be preheated to the required
temperature—if using a fan-assisted oven, cooking times
should be reduced according to the manufacturer's
instructions and guidelines.

contents

introduction

In my ideal world, breakfast and morning treats would be made with love and care, so here are recipes for quick, nutritious weekday breakfasts as well as leisurely weekend brunches. These bakes use nuts and fresh or dried fruit for flavor and nutrition, and are lower in sugar than many of their rich pastry counterparts.

Baking depends on a few key ingredients and their quality determines the result. Luckily, even the best—and these are now usually organically grown—are relatively inexpensive: unsalted butter, free-range eggs, stoneground unbleached flour, untreated fruit, organic nuts, cocoa powder, and chocolate. These days major supermarkets have an excellent range of organic foods.

Life can be simpler for the morning baker if you remember to take butter out of the fridge the night before so it is at room temperature when you are ready to cook. Dry ingredients can be weighed and mixed in advance, bakeware prepared, even a special holiday breakfast table can be set ahead of time.

The quickest recipes are favorites with my small children—French toast and cinnamon toast have an enduring appeal and need no advance preparation. Pancakes and waffles are high on our list of instant treats—three generations of my husband's family have grown up on the gruesomely sticky combination of pancakes layered with peanut butter and maple syrup.

Muffins can also be easily assembled. They freeze well and can be reheated; add a fresh fruit compote and yogurt for a really good combination. Muffins and quick breads go well with savories like scrambled or poached eggs, omelets, cold ham, crispy bacon, or warm smoked haddock or—best of all—kippers.

Leftover quick breads are excellent toasted and buttered. Yeast breads and loaf cakes take more time and planning, and baking ahead—this can work to your advantage. They also keep longer, and most freeze well.

bran, carrot, and cardamom muffins

A healthy bran cereal breakfast—but in delicious muffin form, and just packed with spices and plump raisins.

Preheat the oven to 425°F. Put the cereal in a large bowl, add the milk, and let soak for 10 minutes. Lightly beat the eggs and add to the soaked cereal mixture with the melted butter or oil. Stir well.

Add the dry ingredients, then stir quickly and briefly. Do not overmix; the mixture should be lumpy. Stir in the grated carrots and raisins, if using, then spoon into the prepared muffin pan, filling each cup about two-thirds full.

Bake for about 20 minutes until lightly browned and firm to the touch. Let cool in the pan for 1 minute, then turn out onto a wire rack. Eat warm, immediately or within 24 hours. When thoroughly cooled, the muffins can be wrapped then frozen for up to 1 month.

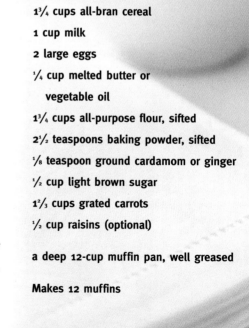

1¾ cups all-bran cereal

1 cup milk

2 large eggs

¼ cup melted butter or
   vegetable oil

1¾ cups all-purpose flour, sifted

2½ teaspoons baking powder, sifted

⅛ teaspoon ground cardamom or ginger

½ cup light brown sugar

1⅓ cups grated carrots

½ cup raisins (optional)

a deep 12-cup muffin pan, well greased

Makes 12 muffins

muffins

Seville orange marmalade—a classic breakfast preserve—adds extra zing to these simple, easy-to-make muffins. Delicous hot or cold.

Preheat the oven to 425°F. Sift the dry ingredients into a large bowl, mix thoroughly, then make a well in the center. Add the egg, milk, orange juice, and oil or melted butter. Stir the marmalade to break up any clumps, then add to the bowl. Mix quickly to form a coarse, slightly streaky batter; do not overmix. Spoon the mixture into the prepared muffin pan, filling each cup about two-thirds full.

Bake for about 20 minutes until lightly browned and firm to the touch. Let cool in the pan for 1 minute, then turn out onto a wire rack. Eat warm, immediately or within 24 hours. When thoroughly cooled, the muffins can be wrapped then frozen for up to 1 month.

1 cup all-purpose flour

1 cup whole-wheat flour

1 tablespoon baking powder

a large pinch of sea salt

1 large egg, lightly beaten

1¼ cups milk

2 teaspoons freshly squeezed orange juice

¼ cup vegetable oil or melted butter

⅔ cup thick-cut Seville orange marmalade

a deep 12-cup muffin pan, well greased

Makes 12 muffins

marmalade muffins

⅓ cup whole blanched almonds

1¾ cups all-purpose flour, sifted

1 tablespoon baking powder, sifted

⅓ cup sugar

grated rind of 1 lemon

1 large egg

1¼ cups milk

2 teaspoons freshly squeezed lemon juice

¼ cup vegetable oil

1 cup fresh blueberries, rinsed and
   thoroughly drained, or frozen blueberries
   (use straight from the freezer)

a deep 12-cup muffin pan, well greased

Makes 12 muffins

Preheat the oven to 400°F. Put the almonds in a food processor or blender, and grind to a coarse meal. They should have more texture than commercially ground almonds. Transfer to a large bowl and mix with the flour, baking powder, sugar, and grated lemon rind.

Lightly beat the egg with the milk, lemon juice, and vegetable oil. Add to the dry ingredients and stir just enough to make a coarse, lumpy mixture. Add the blueberries and mix quickly, using as few strokes as possible, leaving the mixture slightly streaky. Do not beat or overmix or the baked muffins will be tough and dry.

Spoon the mixture into the prepared muffin pan, filling each cup about two-thirds full. Bake for about 20–25 minutes until golden and firm to the touch.

lemon, almond, and blueberry muffins

Let cool in the pan for 1 minute, then turn out onto a wire rack. Eat warm, immediately or within 24 hours. When thoroughly cooled, the muffins can be wrapped then frozen for up to 1 month.

Everyone loves a blueberry muffin. These are extra special, packed with ground almonds. Use wild berries if you can find them.

pecan, orange, and cranberry muffins

1 cup all-purpose flour

1 cup whole-wheat flour

1 tablespoon baking powder

$^1/_3$ cup sugar

$^1/_3$ cup pecans, coarsely chopped

grated rind of $^1/_2$ orange

1 large egg

$1^1/_4$ cups milk

2 teaspoons freshly squeezed
   orange juice

$^1/_4$ cup melted butter or vegetable oil

$1^2/_3$ cups fresh or frozen cranberries
   (use straight from the freezer)

a deep 12-cup muffin pan,
   well greased

Makes 12 muffins

Preheat the oven to 425°F. Sift the flours and baking powder into a large bowl, then stir in the sugar, pecans, and grated orange rind. In another bowl, lightly beat the egg with the milk, orange juice, and melted butter or vegetable oil. Add to the dry ingredients, stirring quickly with a wooden spoon until just mixed. Add the cranberries and stir briefly, using as few strokes as possible. Do not beat or overmix; the batter should look slightly streaky.

Spoon into the prepared muffin pan, filling each cup about two-thirds full. Bake for about 20 minutes until golden brown and firm to the touch. Let cool in the pan for 1 minute, then turn out onto a wire rack. Eat warm, immediately or within 24 hours. When thoroughly cooled, the muffins can be wrapped then frozen for up to 1 month.

fresh peach and oat muffins

1⅓ cups rolled oats

1⅓ cups buttermilk

1 large egg, lightly beaten

⅓ cup melted butter or vegetable oil

½ cup plus 1 tablespoon light brown sugar

1½ cups all-purpose flour

1 teaspoon baking powder

½ teaspoon baking soda

½ teaspoon ground cinnamon

¼ teaspoon freshly grated nutmeg

12 oz. almost ripe peaches, rinsed,
   pitted, and flesh cut into large chunks

a deep 12-cup muffin pan, well greased

Makes 12 muffins

Preheat the oven to 425°F. Put the rolled oats and the buttermilk in a large bowl and let soak for 10 minutes. Add the lightly beaten egg, melted butter or vegetable oil, and sugar and mix well.

Sift the flour, baking powder, baking soda, and spices onto the soaked oat mixture and stir briefly. Quickly fold in the chopped peaches. Do not beat or overmix; the batter should look slightly streaky. Spoon the mixture into the prepared muffin pan, filling each cup about two-thirds full.

Bake for about 20 minutes until golden brown and firm to the touch. Let cool in the pan for 1 minute, then turn out onto a wire rack. Eat warm, immediately or within 24 hours. When thoroughly cooled, the muffins can be wrapped then frozen for up to 1 month.

Fresh peaches make these muffins extra special. Serve warm with fruit salad compote and plenty of plain yogurt.

4 slices bacon, diced

1 cup plus 2 tablespoons yellow cornmeal

1 cup all-purpose flour, sifted

¼ teaspoon coarsely ground black
    pepper or crushed dried chilies

1 tablespoon baking powder

2 large eggs, lightly beaten

1 cup milk

1 tablespoon bacon fat (see recipe),
    vegetable oil, or melted butter

1 teaspoon maple syrup

1 tablespoon fresh herbs, such as snipped
    chives or chopped parsley, or sliced
    scallions

a deep 12-cup muffin pan, well greased

Makes 12 muffins

Preheat the oven to 425°F. Put the bacon into a cold skillet, nonstick if possible, and fry until crisp. Remove the bacon and transfer to a plate lined with crumpled paper towels. Drain off all but 1 tablespoon of the fat in the skillet (if necessary, make up to this amount with vegetable oil or melted butter).

Put all the dry ingredients in a large bowl. Add the bacon, eggs, milk, bacon fat, oil or butter, syrup, and the herbs or scallions. Mix quickly to make a coarse, slightly streaky batter; do not beat or overmix. Spoon the mixture into the prepared muffin pan, filling each cup about two-thirds full. Bake for about 15 minutes until lightly golden and just firm to the touch. Let cool in the pan for 1 minute, then turn out onto a wire rack. Eat warm, immediately or within 24 hours. When thoroughly cooled, the muffins can be wrapped then frozen for up to 1 month.

cornmeal and bacon muffins

Delicious spread with butter and served with scrambled eggs or omelets, cold ham and tomatoes, or a full English fried breakfast.

oat baps

The bap is one of the glories of British baking and in Scotland, the oat capital of the world, they are traditionally made with crunchy oats.

Preheat the oven to 375°F. Put the dry ingredients in a food processor and process to make a fairly coarse mixture. Mix the milk with the lemon juice, then with the machine running, slowly pour enough liquid through the feed tube to make a soft but not sticky dough. Turn out onto a surface dusted with oats, then roll or pat into a round loaf about 9 inches in diameter and ¼ inch thick.

Put the loaf on the prepared baking sheet and, using a sharp knife, score it into 8 wedges. Bake for about 20 minutes until firm and lightly browned underneath. Cool on a wire rack. Eat warm, or split and toast. When thoroughly cooled, the baps can be wrapped then frozen for up to 1 month.

2½ cups steel-cut oats, plus
   extra for dusting

2 cups all-purpose flour, sifted

1 teaspoon sea salt

1 teaspoon baking soda

1¾ cups whole milk or buttermilk

2 teaspoons freshly squeezed
   lemon juice

a large baking sheet, well greased

Makes 8 baps

quick breads

apple buttermilk scone round

Eat warm, spread with butter and lots of apricot preserves, pear and ginger jam, or apple marmalade—a good start to the day.

Preheat the oven to 425°F. Peel, core, and coarsely chop the apple into ½-inch chunks. Mix the flours, baking soda, and sugar in the food processor. Add the butter and process until the mixture looks like fine crumbs. With the machine running, add the buttermilk through the feed tube to make a soft but not sticky dough.

Turn out onto a floured surface and knead in the apple chunks to form a coarse, bumpy dough. Shape into a ball and put in the middle of the prepared baking sheet. With floured fingers, pat the dough into a 9-inch round. Brush lightly with buttermilk or milk to glaze, then sprinkle with a little raw sugar to give a crunchy surface. Using a sharp knife, score the round into 8 wedges. Bake for about 20–25 minutes until golden and firm to the touch.

Cool on a wire rack. Eat warm, immediately or within 24 hours. The scones are also good split and toasted. When thoroughly cooled, they can be wrapped then frozen for up to 1 month.

1 large baking apple or 1–2 crisp tart eating apples (about ½ lb.)

1¾ cups all-purpose flour, plus extra for dusting

¾ cup whole-wheat flour

1 teaspoon baking soda

6½ tablespoons unsalted butter, chilled and diced

½ cup raw sugar, plus extra for sprinkling

about ⅔ cup buttermilk, plus extra for brushing or milk for brushing

a large baking sheet, greased

Makes 8 scones

irish breakfast bread

2½ cups whole-wheat flour

¾ cup all-purpose flour

1 teaspoon baking soda

1 teaspoon sea salt

2 tablespoons sesame seeds

1 teaspoon light brown sugar

1 teaspoon ground ginger

2 tablespoons unsalted butter,
   chilled and diced

1 large egg

1⅓ cups plain yogurt

1½ tablespoons molasses

1 tablespoon sesame seeds

an 8½ x 4½ x 2½ inch loaf pan,
   well greased

Makes 1 medium loaf

Preheat the oven to 400°F. Put the flours and baking soda in a large bowl, then stir in the salt, sesame seeds, sugar, and ginger. Mix well. Rub in the chilled cubes of butter with your fingertips until the mixture looks like fine crumbs.

Lightly beat the egg with the yogurt and molasses, then quickly stir into the dry mixture, using a wooden spoon. With floured hands, knead the dough 2–3 times in the bowl so it just comes together. It should be heavy and sticky— quite unlike a scone dough or a yeast bread dough. If it is too dry or too wet, add extra yogurt or flour, 1 tablespoon at a time. (The exact amount of liquid needed will depend on the quality of the flour.) Shape the dough into a loaf to fit the pan, then gently roll it in the sesame seeds to cover. Press the dough neatly into the prepared pan.

Bake the loaf for 10 minutes, then reduce temperature to 350°F and bake for 35 minutes more. (If it browns too quickly or too much, cover with foil.) The baked bread should be browned, well risen, and should sound hollow when turned out and tapped underneath. If it sounds heavy or the crust is flabby, return the turned-out loaf to the oven for 5 minutes, then test again.

Cool on a wire rack. Although this loaf is good the day it is baked, it tastes even better if wrapped and kept for a day before eating. When thoroughly cooled, the loaf can be wrapped then frozen for up to 1 month.

Cottage cheese gives these rolls a rich dairy flavor—perfect for breakfast. Add fresh herbs or dried fruit for a wonderful variation.

2½ cups self-rising flour, sifted, plus
    extra for dusting
½ teaspoon sea salt
1¼ cups cottage cheese or ricotta
1 large egg
about ⅔ cup milk
extra milk or beaten egg, for glazing

Herb rolls:
3 tablespoons chopped parsley
¼ teaspoon freshly ground black pepper

Fruit rolls:
2 tablespoons sugar
    or 1 tablespoon honey
3 tablespoons dried sour cherries,
    cranberries, or fresh blueberries

a large baking sheet, floured

Makes 10 rolls

Preheat the oven to 375°F. Put the flour, salt, cottage cheese or ricotta, and egg in a food processor and whiz until just mixed. With the machine running, add enough milk through the feed tube until the mixture comes together to form a soft but not sticky dough.

Turn out onto a lightly floured surface and knead lightly 2—3 times until smooth. Divide the dough into 10 equal pieces and shape each one into a ball. Arrange, spaced slightly apart, on the floured baking sheet and brush lightly with milk or beaten egg. Bake for about 20 minutes until golden brown and firm to the touch. Cool on a wire rack. Eat warm, immediately or within 24 hours, or split and toast. When thoroughly cooled, the rolls can be wrapped then frozen for up to 1 month.

Variations:
Herb rolls: Add the parsley and pepper to the processor with the other ingredients, then proceed with the recipe.
Fruit rolls: Add the sugar or honey to the processor with the flour. Make the dough, as above. Knead the fruit into it. Proceed as above.

cottage cheese rolls

The traditional bread of Ireland: this variation uses mixed-grains flour for extra flavor. Perfect with smoked salmon and scrambled eggs.

brown soda bread

2½ cups mixed-grains flour

⅔ cup all-purpose flour, sifted, plus
   extra for dusting

1 teaspoon sea salt

1 teaspoon baking soda, sifted

1 tablespoon unsalted butter, chilled and
   diced

1¼–1½ cups buttermilk or plain yogurt

a baking sheet, well floured

Makes 1 medium loaf

Preheat the oven to 425°F. Put the flours, salt, and baking soda in a large bowl. Rub in the diced butter with your fingertips until the mixture looks like fine crumbs. Make a well in the center and, using a spatula or wooden spoon, work in enough buttermilk or yogurt to form a coarse, stiff dough. Turn out onto a floured surface and knead 2–3 times. Shape into a round loaf about 7 inches across and 1¼ inches thick. Put on the baking sheet and dust lightly with flour. Cut a fairly deep cross on the surface of the loaf, then bake for about 25–30 minutes until well risen with a good,

browned crust. The bread should sound hollow when tapped underneath. Cool on a wire rack. Eat within 24 hours, or split and toast. When thoroughly cooled, the soda bread can be wrapped then frozen for up to 1 month.

Variations:

Fruit soda bread: Follow the main recipe, replacing the mixed-grains flour with stoneground whole-wheat flour. Add 1 tablespoon brown sugar and ¾ cup mixed dried fruit to the rubbed-in mixture, then add the buttermilk and proceed as above.

Spotted soda bread: Follow the recipe for fruit soda bread, using 1 cup coarsely chopped bittersweet chocolate (choose one with 50–58 percent cocoa solids) instead of the dried fruit.

a large pinch of saffron strands

3–4 tablespoons cold milk

1¾ cups self-rising flour, sifted

a pinch of salt

2 tablespoons sugar

3½ tablespoons unsalted butter, chilled and diced

1 large egg

extra milk or beaten egg, to glaze

a 2½-inch plain or fluted cookie cutter

a baking sheet, lightly greased

Makes 8 scones

For the lightest, fluffiest scones, make them in a food processor and handle the mixture as little as possible. Eat with butter and honey.

Preheat the oven to 350°F. Put the saffron in a small heatproof dish and toast in the oven for 10–15 minutes until slightly darkened but not scorched. Let cool for 1 minute, then crumble the strands back into the dish, add 2 tablespoons of the milk, cover and let soak overnight or at least 4 hours.

Increase oven temperature to 425°F. Mix the flour, salt, and sugar in a food processor. Add the butter and process until the mixture looks like fine crumbs. Beat the egg with the saffron milk, then with the machine running, slowly pour the liquid through the feed tube to bring the mixture together to make a soft but not sticky dough. If the dough seems dry and won't come together, add 1–2 tablespoons milk. Turn out onto a lightly floured surface, then pat or roll out to about 1 inch thick. Dip the cookie cutter in flour and stamp out as many rounds as possible. Gather the trimmings into a ball, pat out again, and cut out more rounds. Repeat until all the dough has been used.

Put the scones well apart on the baking sheet. They can be left plain, dusted lightly with flour, or glazed with a little milk or beaten egg. Bake for about 12 minutes until risen, golden, and just firm. Cool on a wire rack. Eat warm, or split and toast. When thoroughly cooled, the scones can be wrapped then frozen for up to 1 month.

Variation:

Blue cheese scones: Omit the sugar. Knead ½ cup crumbled Stilton or Shropshire Blue cheese (avoid Danish Blue as it is too salty) into the dough with ½ cup walnut pieces, then continue as above.

saffron scones

french toast

4 slices thick-cut white bread, challah, or brioche

2 large eggs, beaten

2 tablespoons light cream or half-and-half

½ teaspoon pure vanilla extract

3½ tablespoons sugar

about 2 tablespoons butter, for sautéing

½ teaspoon ground cinnamon

maple syrup, to serve (optional)

Serves 4

Trim the crusts from the bread, then cut the slices in half. Put the eggs, cream, vanilla extract, and 1 teaspoon of the sugar in a shallow dish and mix with a fork.

Heat half the butter in a large, heavy, cast iron or nonstick skillet. When the butter is foaming, briefly dip a piece of bread in the egg mixture until thoroughly coated, drain off the excess, and put it in the hot butter. Add 3 more pieces to the skillet in the same way, then cook over a medium heat for about 3–4 minutes until the underside is golden brown. Turn the bread over and cook the other side. Meanwhile, mix the remaining sugar and cinnamon in a small sugar shaker or small bowl. Put the cooked bread on a warm serving plate and sprinkle with some of the cinnamon sugar.

Wipe out the skillet and reheat. Add the rest of the butter and cook the other pieces of bread as before. Serve hot as soon as possible, sprinkled with more cinnamon sugar and maple syrup, if using.

cinnamon toast

The quickest, simplest breakfast treat ever invented, but it does demand top-quality ingredients—good white bread, unsalted butter, and the best ground cinnamon.

Heat the broiler, toast thick slices of bread on both sides, then butter thoroughly. Mix the cinnamon sugar, as in the previous recipe, and sprinkle generously to cover. Put the toast back under the broiler until the sugar starts to melt and bubble. Remove carefully and eat when the toast has cooled enough not to burn your lips (the top will look like a brandy snap—lacy and crisp).

pancakes

Sift the flour, salt, and sugar into a bowl, then make a well in the center. Add the egg yolks, butter, and milk and beat with a whisk until mixed. Gradually work in the flour to make a very thick but lump-free batter. In another bowl, beat the egg whites until stiff, then fold them into the batter with a large metal spoon. Heat a heavy-bottom skillet until medium hot, then grease it lightly with butter.

Sauté the mixture in batches of 3, using a heaping tablespoon of batter for each pancake. Cook for 1 minute until golden underneath, then turn over with a spatula and cook for another minute. Eat hot with maple syrup.

¾ cup plus 2 tablespoons all-purpose flour

a good pinch of salt

1 tablespoon sugar

2 large eggs, separated

1 tablespoon butter, melted, plus extra for cooking

¾ cup plus 1 tablespoon whole milk

maple syrup, to serve

Makes 12 pancakes

Serves 4

waffles

Make the batter as for the pancakes, but use just 1 egg and add 1½ teaspoons baking powder with the flour and ½ teaspoon of pure vanilla extract with the milk.

Crisp waffles or fluffy, thick pancakes drizzled with maple syrup make a good breakfast.

Using a non-plastic pastry brush, thoroughly grease a waffle iron or electric waffle maker with a little melted butter, then heat (according to the maker's instructions). Pour in enough batter to fill, then close and cook over medium heat for 30 seconds. Turn the waffle iron over and cook the other side for 30 seconds. For an electric waffle maker, follow the manufacturer's guidelines for cooking. Dust the hot waffles with confectioners' sugar and eat immediately, drizzled with maple syrup, or omit the confectioners' sugar and serve with eggs and bacon.

Serves 4

Drinking coffee, chatting with friends, and eating cake—perfect.

1 stick unsalted butter, at room temperature

1 cup light brown sugar

1¾ cups all-purpose flour

2 teaspoons baking soda

2 large eggs

1 cup plus 1 tablespoon sour cream

Filling and topping:

3 tablespoons dark brown sugar

1 tablespoon ground cinnamon

1 cup walnut pieces

a 9½ x 5½ x 3½ inch loaf pan, greased and lined with waxed paper or parchment

Makes 1 large loaf cake

Preheat the oven to 350°F. Using an electric mixer or wooden spoon, beat the butter until light and creamy. Add the sugar—sift it first if it appears lumpy—and beat again until light and fluffy. Sift the flour and baking soda onto the creamed butter mixture. Stir once or twice, then quickly beat the eggs with the sour cream and add to the bowl. Using a rubber spatula or wooden spoon, stir all the ingredients together to make a soft, smooth batter.

Mix the filling and topping ingredients. Spoon half of the cake batter into the prepared loaf pan, then sprinkle over half the filling and topping mixture. Spoon the rest of the cake batter on top and smooth the surface. Sprinkle over the rest of the filling and topping mixture, then press lightly onto the surface of the loaf.

Bake for about 45 minutes to 1 hour until lightly browned and firm and a skewer inserted into the center comes out clean. Let cool in the pan for 5 minutes, then carefully turn out onto a wire rack. Serve warm. The cake is best eaten within 3 days. When thoroughly cooled, the loaf cake can be wrapped then frozen for up to 1 month.

sour cream coffee cake

loaf cakes

Light and crumbly in texture, crammed with delicious fruit and nuts—irresistible. Use very ripe bananas for maximum flavor.

banana pecan loaf

Preheat the oven to 350°F. Using an electric mixer or wooden spoon, beat the butter with the sugar until light and creamy. Gradually beat in the eggs and vanilla to make a fluffy mixture. Mash the bananas with a fork—they should be fairly coarse rather than a purée. Carefully fold in the mashed bananas, pecans, and flour. Transfer the mixture to the prepared pan and smooth the surface with a spatula. Bake for about 1 hour until golden and firm to the touch and a skewer inserted into the center comes out clean.

Let cool in the pan for 5 minutes, then turn out onto a wire rack to cool completely. Serve warm or at room temperature, thickly sliced and spread with butter. The cake is best eaten within 3 days. When thoroughly cooled, it can be wrapped then frozen for up to 1 month.

1 stick plus 2 teaspoons unsalted butter, at room temperature

$\frac{3}{4}$ cup plus 2 teaspoons sugar

2 large eggs, beaten

$\frac{1}{2}$ teaspoon pure vanilla extract

3 small very ripe bananas, peeled

1 cup pecans, coarsely sliced

2 cups less 1 tablespoon self-rising flour, sifted

a $9\frac{1}{2}$ x $5\frac{1}{2}$ x $3\frac{1}{2}$ inch loaf pan, greased and lined with waxed paper or parchment

Makes 1 large loaf cake

country apple cake

I adore the simple, fresh taste in this easy loaf cake—perfect when you need an energy boost and crave something uncomplicated.

Preheat the oven to 350°F. Using an electirc mixer or wooden spoon, beat the butter until creamy, then add the sugar and beat until light and fluffy. Gradually beat in the eggs, then the vanilla. Using a large metal spoon, fold in the flour and enough milk to make a soft mixture that just drops from the spoon. Transfer the mixture to the prepared loaf pan and smooth the surface with a spatula. Arrange an even layer of apple slices over the top.

To make the topping, put all the ingredients in a bowl and rub together with your fingertips until the mixture looks like coarse crumbs. (The ingredients can also be mixed in a food processor.) Sprinkle the topping evenly over the apples, then press down gently to firm. Bake for about 1 hour until golden and a skewer inserted into the center comes out clean.

Let cool in the pan until lukewarm, then serve warm from the pan or cool completely on a wire rack. Eat within 3 days. When thoroughly cooled, the loaf cake can be wrapped then frozen for up to 1 month.

7 tablespoons unsalted butter, at room temperature

1/2 cup plus 1 tablespoon sugar

2 large eggs, beaten

1/2 teaspoon pure vanilla extract

1 cup self-rising flour, sifted

2–3 tablespoons milk

1 1/2 cups thickly sliced tart eating apples

Topping:

1/2 cup raw sugar

6 1/2 tablespoons unsalted butter, chilled and diced

1 cup all-purpose flour, sifted

an 8 1/2 x 4 1/2 x 2 1/2 inch loaf pan, greased and lined with waxed paper or parchment

Makes 1 medium loaf cake

1 firm, slightly underripe pear

1²⁄₃ cups self-rising flour

1 teaspoon baking soda

1 tablespoon ground ginger

1 teaspoon ground cinnamon

1 teaspoon apple-pie spice

¹⁄₈ teaspoon ground black pepper

1 stick unsalted butter, chilled and diced

¹⁄₂ cup molasses

¹⁄₂ cup light corn syrup

²⁄₃ cup dark brown sugar

1¹⁄₄ cups milk

1 large egg, beaten

a 9¹⁄₂ x 5¹⁄₂ x 3¹⁄₂ inch loaf pan, greased and lined with waxed paper or parchment

Makes 1 large loaf cake

Preheat the oven to 350°F. Peel, core, and dice the pear into ¹⁄₂-inch pieces. Set aside. Sift the flour, baking soda, and spices into a bowl. Rub in the diced butter with your fingertips until the mixture looks like fine crumbs. Alternatively, use a food processor.

Put the molasses and corn syrup in a small saucepan, melt over low heat, then cool until lukewarm. Dissolve the sugar in the milk over low heat, stirring frequently, then let cool until lukewarm.

Beat the milk into the flour mixture, quickly followed by the molasses mixture and the egg. When smooth and lump-free, pour the mixture into the prepared loaf pan. Top with the diced pear—the pieces will slowly sink as they cook.

Bake the gingerbread for 45 minutes to 1 hour until well risen and firm to the touch and a skewer inserted into the center comes out clean. Let cool completely in the pan, then turn out. Serve warm or at room temperature, thickly sliced. The gingerbread is best eaten within 2 days and is not suitable for freezing.

pear gingerbread

Pears and ginger go hand-in-hand in this deliciously rich cake.

For a full tea flavor, use a strong variety such as English or Irish blend, or a rich malty Assam. Eat the loaf cake thickly sliced, warm or even toasted, with or without butter and jam.

breakfast tea loaf

2 cups all-bran cereal

²/₃ cup dark brown sugar

1 cup mix of raisins, golden raisins, and
   currants

³/₄ cup plus 1 tablespoon freshly brewed tea,
   warm

¹/₃ cup walnut pieces

³/₄ cup all-purpose flour, sifted

1¹/₂ teaspoons baking powder

1¹/₂ teaspoons apple-pie spice

an 8¹/₂ x 4¹/₂ x 2¹/₂ inch loaf pan, greased
   and lined with waxed paper or parchment

Makes 1 medium loaf cake

Preheat the oven to 350°F. Put the cereal, sugar, and dried fruit into a large bowl, pour the warm tea over, stir well, then cover and let soak for 30 minutes.

Add the remaining ingredients, and stir with a wooden spoon until thoroughly mixed. (The cereal will disappear into the mixture.)

Spoon the mixture into the prepared loaf pan and smooth the surface with a spatula. Bake for about 45 minutes until firm and well risen and a skewer or wooden toothpick inserted into the center comes out clean.

Let cool in the pan until lukewarm, then turn out and eat while still warm. Alternatively, turn out onto a wire rack to cool completely.

The tea loaf is best if wrapped and kept for a day before cutting. Eat within 4 days, or wrap then freeze for up to 1 month.

carrot and almond loaf cake

Everyone loves a carrot cake—this one is moist and packed with creamy, crunchy almonds. Delicious any time of the morning.

Preheat the oven to 350°F. Put the flour, all the almonds, lemon rind, and carrots in a large bowl and mix with a wooden spoon.

Beat the egg yolks with half the sugar until very thick and fluffy. In another, spotlessly clean, grease-free bowl, beat the egg whites until stiff peaks form, then gradually beat in the sugar to form a meringue. Using a large metal spoon, gently fold the carrot mixture into the beaten yolk mixture, followed by the meringue. (There should be no trace of meringue visible in the mixture.)

Spoon the mixture into the prepared loaf pan and smooth the surface. Bake for about 1 hour until golden and firm to the touch and a skewer inserted into the center comes out clean. Let cool in the pan until lukewarm, then turn out onto a wire rack to cool completely. The loaf cake is best eaten within 2 days and is not suitable for freezing.

²/₃ cup self-rising flour, sifted

3 cups ground almonds

¹/₃ cup whole blanched almonds, very coarsely ground, or slivered almonds

grated rind of 1 small lemon

2 cups grated carrots (about 9 oz. before peeling and trimming)

6 large eggs, separated

1¹/₃ cups light brown sugar

a 9¹/₂ x 5¹/₂ x 3¹/₂ inch loaf pan, greased and lined with waxed paper or parchment

Makes 1 large loaf cake

les petits pains au lait

Gently heat the butter, honey, and milk in a small saucepan until the butter melts. Let cool until lukewarm, then crumble in the yeast and beat until smooth. Mix the flour and salt in a large bowl, then make a well in the center. Pour in the yeast liquid and the eggs, then work in the flour to make a soft but not sticky dough. If it is is too dry or too sticky, add extra water or flour, 1 tablespoon at a time. Turn out onto a lightly floured surface and knead thoroughly for 10 minutes (or 6 minutes at medium speed in a mixer fitted with a dough hook). Return the dough to the bowl and cover with a damp cloth or put the bowl in an oiled plastic bag. Let rise at room temperature until doubled in size—about 2 hours.

Punch down the risen dough with your knuckles, turn out, and knead lightly. Cut into 16 even-sized pieces and shape into ovals, 4 x 2½ x ½ inches. Set well apart on the baking sheets, cover, and let rise as before until doubled in size— about 1 hour. Preheat the oven to 425°F. Brush the rolls with beaten egg or milk to glaze and sprinkle with the sugar. Using a sharp knife, make a long shallow slit down the length of each one. Bake for 12–15 minutes until the rolls are browned and sound hollow when tapped underneath. Cool on a wire rack. Eat warm, immediately or within 24 hours, or split and toast. When thoroughly cooled, the rolls can be wrapped then frozen for up to 1 month.

To use dry yeast, mix one ¼ oz. packet with the flour and salt. Make a well in the center, add the butter, milk, and honey mixture and eggs, then proceed with the recipe.

6 tablespoons unsalted butter

1½ tablespoons honey

1½ cups milk

1 cake compressed yeast (0.6 oz.)*

5¼ cups unbleached white bread flour, sifted

2 teaspoons sea salt

3 large eggs, beaten

extra beaten egg or milk, for brushing

raw sugar, for sprinkling

2 large baking sheets, greased

Makes 16 rolls

yeast breads

Great for a fast, simple breakfast—on its own or toasted and buttered. Cinnamon, raisins, and nuts are a classic combination.

4 cups unbleached white bread flour

1½ tablespoons ground cinnamon

1 teaspoon sea salt

1 teaspoon light brown sugar

7 tablespoons butter, chilled and diced

1 cake compressed yeast (0.6 oz.)*

1¾ cups milk, at room temperature

⅔ cup raisins

¾ cup walnut pieces, lightly toasted

a large baking sheet, greased

Makes 1 large loaf

cinnamon raisin nut bread

Sift the flour, cinnamon, salt, and sugar into a large bowl. Rub in the butter with your fingertips until the mixture looks like fine crumbs, then make a well in the center. Crumble the yeast into a pitcher and beat in the milk. Pour into the well and mix in enough flour to make a thick batter. Cover the bowl and leave until thick and foamy—about 20 minutes.

Work in the rest of the flour to make a soft but not sticky dough. If it is too dry or too sticky, add extra water or flour, 1 tablespoon at a time. Turn out onto a floured surface and knead thoroughly for 10 minutes (or 6 minutes at medium speed in a mixer fitted with a dough hook) until smooth and elastic. Return to the bowl, cover with a damp cloth, and let rise at room temperature until doubled in size—about 1½ hours.

Punch down the risen dough with your knuckles, then work in the raisins and nuts, kneading until thoroughly mixed. Shape the dough into an oval loaf, 10 x 6 inches. Put on the prepared baking sheet, cover, and let rise as before until doubled in size—about 45 minutes.

Preheat the oven to 425°F. Bake for 35 minutes until the bread is browned and sounds hollow when tapped underneath. Cool on a wire rack. Eat within 4 days, or slice and toast. When thoroughly cooled, the loaf can be wrapped then frozen for up to 1 month.

To use dry yeast, mix one ¼ oz. packet with ⅓ cup of the sifted flour mixture. Mix to a thick batter with the milk, cover, and leave until thick and foamy. Rub the butter into the remaining flour, add the frothy yeast mixture, and proceed with the recipe.

sticky buns

Mix the flour, salt, and sugar in a large bowl and make a well in the center. Crumble the yeast into another bowl, add the lukewarm milk, and stir until blended. Pour the yeast liquid into the well, then work in enough of the flour to make a thick batter. Cover the bowl with a damp cloth and leave until foamy, thick, and full of air bubbles—about 15 minutes.

Add the butter and egg to the yeast mixture and work in the rest of the flour to make a soft but not sticky dough. If it is too dry or too sticky, add extra water or flour, 1 tablespoon at a time. Turn out onto a lightly floured surface and knead thoroughly for 10 minutes (or 6 minutes at medium speed in a mixer fitted with a dough hook). Return to the bowl and cover with a damp cloth or put it in an oiled plastic bag. Let rise at room temperature until doubled in size—about 1½ hours.

Punch down the risen dough with your knuckles, then turn out and roll out to a rectangle, about 16 x 10 inches. To make the filling, beat the butter until creamy, then beat in the cinnamon and sugar. Spread the mixture over the dough leaving a ¼-inch border around the edges. Scatter the nuts over, then roll into a 16-inch-long roll. Cut into 12 equal pieces and space slightly apart in the prepared loaf pan, in 4 rows of 3. Cover and let rise as before until doubled in size—about 30 minutes (or overnight in the refrigerator). Preheat the oven to 400°F.

Put the topping ingredients in a small saucepan, bring to a boil, reduce the heat, and simmer for 1 minute. Pour the hot mixture over the buns. Bake for about 25–30 minutes until golden and firm. Let cool in the pan for about 10 minutes, then turn out carefully—the caramel will be hot. Cool on a wire rack. Eat warm or at room temperature, within 24 hours. The buns are not suitable for freezing.

To use dry yeast mix one ¼ oz. packet with ⅓ cup of the flour. Mix with the warm milk and leave until thick and foamy. Mix the remaining flour with the sugar and salt in a bowl, add the frothy yeast mixture, egg, and butter, then proceed with the recipe.

An all-time family favorite. Who can resist these gooey, sticky caramel buns filled with cinnamon and nuts?

3½ cups unbleached white bread flour, sifted

1 teaspoon sea salt

2 tablespoons sugar

1 cake compressed yeast (0.6 oz.)*

about ¾ cup plus 1 tablespoon milk,
    lukewarm

6 tablespoons unsalted butter, melted

1 large egg, beaten

Nut caramel filling:

5 tablespoons unsalted butter, very soft

2 teaspoons ground cinnamon

⅓ cup light brown sugar

1 cup pecans or walnut halves or pieces

Sticky topping:

½ cup plus 1 tablespoon light brown sugar

¼ cup heavy cream

a 9 x 11 x 1¾ inch baking or roasting pan,
    well greased

Makes 12 buns

sour cherry brioche

3¹⁄₂ cups unbleached white bread flour, sifted

1¹⁄₂ teaspoons sea salt

1 cake compressed yeast (0.6 oz.)*

2¹⁄₂ tablespoons milk, lukewarm

6 large eggs, beaten

1³⁄₄ sticks unsalted butter, very soft

3 tablespoons sugar

¹⁄₂ cup dried sour cherries

extra beaten egg or milk, to glaze

a 9-inch springform pan, well greased

Makes 1 large loaf

Mix the flour and salt in an electric mixer or a large bowl. Make a
well in the center. Crumble the yeast into a large measuring pitcher,
beat in the lukewarm milk until smooth, then beat in the eggs.
Pour into the well and mix with a dough hook or by hand to make
a smooth, soft, and sticky dough. Knead until firm, silky, and very
elastic—about 6–7 minutes with a dough hook on medium-low
speed, or 10 minutes by hand. Cover with a damp cloth, or upside-
down bowl and let rest for 10 minutes.

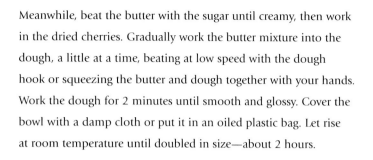

Meanwhile, beat the butter with the sugar until creamy, then work in the dried cherries. Gradually work the butter mixture into the dough, a little at a time, beating at low speed with the dough hook or squeezing the butter and dough together with your hands. Work the dough for 2 minutes until smooth and glossy. Cover the bowl with a damp cloth or put it in an oiled plastic bag. Let rise at room temperature until doubled in size—about 2 hours.

Punch down the risen dough with your knuckles to flatten, cover, and chill for at least 12 hours or overnight. The dough must be thoroughly chilled or it will be difficult to handle and shape.

Turn out the dough onto a lightly floured surface and divide into 18 equal pieces. Shape into neat balls and arrange in the prepared pan to resemble a crown. Cover and let rise as before until doubled in size—about 45 minutes to 1 hour. Preheat the oven to 425°F.

To glaze the brioche, brush it with beaten egg or milk. Bake for about 35 minutes until well risen, golden brown, and firm. It should sound hollow when turned out and tapped underneath. (If it browns too quickly or too much, cover with foil or baking parchment.) Cool on a wire rack. Serve warm, within 2 days, or slice and toast. When thoroughly cooled, the brioche can be wrapped then frozen for up to 1 month.

To use dry yeast, mix one ¼ oz. packet with the flour and salt. Whisk the eggs and milk together, then proceed with the recipe.

Halve the apricots, then put them in a heatproof bowl with the honey and pour over ⅔ cup very hot water. Stir, then set aside and leave, uncovered, until the water is tepid and the honey has dissolved.

Mix the flours in a large bowl and add the salt. Make a well in the center. Crumble the yeast into a small pitcher and beat in the milk until blended. Pour into the well with the melted butter or oil, then add the apricots and their soaking liquid. Mix in the flour to make a soft but not sticky dough. If the dough is too dry or too sticky, add extra water or flour, 1 tablespoon at a time.

Work in the hazelnuts, then turn out the dough onto a lightly floured surface and knead thoroughly for 10 minutes. Return to the bowl and cover with a damp cloth or put the bowl in an oiled plastic bag. Let rise at room temperature until doubled in size —about 1½ hours. Punch down the risen dough with your knuckles, then turn out onto a work surface dusted with rye flour. Shape into a loaf and press gently into the pan. Cover and let rise as before at room temperature until doubled in size—about 1 hour. Preheat the oven to 425°F.

Bake for 35–40 minutes until the loaf is golden brown and sounds hollow when turned out and tapped underneath. Cool on a wire rack. The bread is best eaten within 4 days, or sliced and toasted. Serve with butter, preserves, honey, or cheese. When thoroughly cooled, the loaf can be wrapped then frozen for up to 1 month.

¾ cup dried apricots

2 tablespoons clover honey

2⅔ cups unbleached white bread flour

⅔ cup rye flour, plus extra for dusting

2 teaspoons sea salt

1 cake compressed yeast (0.6 oz.)*

⅔ cup milk, at room temperature

2 tablespoons melted butter or olive oil

¾ cup hazelnuts, toasted and halved

a 9½ x 5½ x 3½ inch loaf pan, greased

Makes 1 large loaf

To use dry yeast, mix one ¼ oz. packet with the flours and salt. Add the milk, butter, and apricot mixture, then proceed with the recipe.

apricot and honey rye bread

Delicious lightly buttered and topped with honey, preserves, or cheese.

double chocolate kugelhopf

A pretty, very rich yeast cake from Austria, Germany, and Alsace—a luxurious breakfast or mid-morning snack.

To make the nut coating, thickly butter the inside of the mold (glazed earthenware, nonstick, heatproof glass, or metal), then press the almonds all around. Chill while you prepare the cake dough.

To make the cake dough, sift the flour, cocoa, salt, and sugar into a large bowl and make a well in the center. Crumble the yeast into a small bowl and beat in the lukewarm milk to make a smooth liquid. Pour into the well, then work in enough of the flour to make a thick batter. Cover with a damp cloth or put it in an oiled plastic bag and leave at room temperature for about 30 minutes. The batter should be bubbly and thick.

Add the eggs to the batter, mix well, then gradually beat in the flour to make a soft, very sticky dough. Beat the

2⅓ cups unbleached white bread flour
½ cup unsweetened cocoa powder
½ teaspoon sea salt
½ cup plus 1 tablespoon sugar
1 cake compressed yeast (0.6 oz.)*
¾ cup plus 2 tablespoons milk, lukewarm
3 large eggs, at room temperature, beaten
7 tablespoons unsalted butter, very soft
⅓ cup slivered almonds
2½ oz. white chocolate, coarsely chopped
confectioners' sugar, for dusting

Nut coating:
2 tablespoons unsalted butter, very soft
⅓ cup slivered almonds

a 9-inch kugelhopf mold

Makes 1 large cake

dough in the bowl using your hand or with the dough hook in an electric mixer for about 5 minutes or until firm, smooth, very elastic, and shiny. Work in the butter, a little at a time, until thoroughly incorporated, then work in the almonds and white chocolate. When evenly mixed, carefully spoon the soft dough into the prepared kugelhopf mold. It should be half-full.

Cover the mold with a damp cloth or put it in an oiled plastic bag and let rise at room temperature until the dough has risen to about 1 inch below the rim—about 1 hour. Preheat the oven to 400°F.

Bake the kugelhopf for about 45 minutes or until a skewer inserted into the cake, midway between the outer edge and inner tube, comes out clean. Let cool for 2 minutes, then carefully turn out onto a wire rack and let cool completely. Serve dusted with confectioners' sugar. It is best eaten within 3 days, or sliced and lightly toasted. When thoroughly cooled, the kugelhopf can be wrapped then frozen for up to 1 month.

To use dry yeast, mix one ¼ oz. packet with about 1 cup of the flour mixture. Mix in the milk to make a smooth batter, cover and leave for about 30 minutes until thick and foamy. Make a well in the remaining flour mixture, add the frothy yeast mixture and eggs, then proceed with the recipe.

1 teaspoon saffron strands

3½ cups unbleached white bread flour,
  sifted

1 teaspoon sea salt

1 stick plus 5 tablespoons unsalted
  butter, chilled and diced

1 cake compressed yeast (0.6 oz.)*

¾ cup milk, lukewarm, plus extra,
  for brushing

2 tablespoons honey

a 9½ x 5½ x 3½ inch loaf pan, greased

Makes 1 large loaf

saffron and honey bread

Well-flavored but not over-sweet—wonderful spread with butter and fruit preserves, or toasted and served with ham and eggs.

Preheat the oven to 350°F. Put the saffron in a small heatproof dish and toast in the oven for 10–15 minutes until darkened but not scorched. Let cool, then add 3 tablespoons water, cover, and let soak overnight.

The next day, mix the flour and salt in a large bowl. Rub in the diced butter with your fingertips until the mixture looks like fine crumbs. Make a well in the center. Crumble the yeast into a small pitcher, then beat in the milk and honey to make a smooth liquid. Pour into the well, followed by the saffron liquid. Mix with your hand to make a soft but not sticky dough.

Turn out onto a floured surface and knead thoroughly for 10 minutes (or 6 minutes at medium speed in a mixer fitted with a dough hook) until smooth, silky, and elastic. Return to the bowl, cover with a damp cloth or put it in an oiled plastic bag and let rise at room temperature until doubled in size—about 1½ hours.

Punch down the risen dough with your knuckles, turn out onto a lightly floured surface and shape into a loaf to fit the pan. Press the dough neatly into the prepared pan. Cover and let rise as before until doubled in size—about 1 hour. Preheat the oven to 375°F.

Brush the risen loaf with milk, then bake for 30 minutes until lightly browned. Reduce the oven temperature to 350°F and bake for 15–20 minutes more, until the turned-out loaf sounds hollow when tapped underneath. (If it browns too quickly or too much, cover with foil or parchment.) Cool on a wire rack. It is best eaten within 4 days, or sliced and toasted. When thoroughly cooled, the loaf can be wrapped then frozen for up to 1 month.

To use dry yeast, mix one ¼ oz. packet with the flour and salt, rub in the butter to look like fine crumbs, add the milk and honey, then proceed with the recipe.

5¼ cups unbleached white bread flour, sifted,
   plus extra, for dusting
3 teaspoons sea salt
1 cake compressed yeast (0.6 oz.)*
about 2 cups buttermilk, at room temperature

a large baking sheet, greased

Makes 1 large loaf

Cultured buttermilk gives white flour a distinctive tang. This loaf has rustic, country appeal.

Put the flour and salt in a large bowl and make a well in the center. Crumble the yeast into a small bowl, mix to a smooth paste with 1 tablespoon lukewarm water, then stir in the buttermilk. Pour the yeast liquid into the well and gradually work in the flour to make a soft dough. If the dough is too sticky or too dry, add more flour or lukewarm water, 1 tablespoon at a time.

Turn out the dough onto a floured surface and knead thoroughly for 10 minutes (or 6 minutes at medium speed in a mixer fitted with a dough hook) until smooth, silky, and elastic. Return to the bowl, cover with a damp cloth and let rise at room temperature until doubled in size —about 1½ hours.

Punch down the risen dough with your knuckles. Turn out onto a lighly floured surface, knead briefly, and shape into a ball. Lightly dust with flour. Put on the prepared baking sheet, cover, and let rise as before until doubled in size—45 minutes to 1 hour. Preheat the oven to 425°F. Using a very sharp knife, score the top in a criss-cross pattern, as pictured. Bake for 40 minutes until the loaf is golden and sounds hollow when tapped underneath. Cool on a wire rack. It is best eaten within 3 days, or sliced and toasted. When thoroughly cooled, the loaf can be wrapped then frozen for up to 1 month.

*To use dry yeast, mix one ¼ oz. packet with the flour and salt, then proceed with the recipe.

buttermilk hedgehog loaf

conversion chart

Weights and measures have been rounded up
or down slightly to make measuring easier.

volume equivalents:

american	metric	imperial
1 teaspoon	5 ml	
1 tablespoon	15 ml	
¼ cup	60 ml	2 fl.oz.
⅓ cup	75 ml	2½ fl.oz.
½ cup	125 ml	4 fl.oz.
⅔ cup	150 ml	5 fl.oz. (¼ pint)
¾ cup	175 ml	6 fl.oz.
1 cup	250 ml	8 fl.oz.

weight equivalents: measurements:

imperial	metric	inches	cm
1 oz.	25 g	¼ inch	5 mm
2 oz.	50 g	½ inch	1 cm
3 oz.	75 g	¾ inch	1.5 cm
4 oz.	125 g	1 inch	2.5 cm
5 oz.	150 g	2 inches	5 cm
6 oz.	175 g	3 inches	7 cm
7 oz.	200 g	4 inches	10 cm
8 oz.	250 g	5 inches	12 cm
9 oz.	275 g	6 inches	15 cm
10 oz.	300 g	7 inches	18 cm
11 oz.	325 g	8 inches	20 cm
12 oz.	375 g	9 inches	23 cm
13 oz.	400 g	10 inches	25 cm
14 oz.	425 g	11 inches	28 cm
15 oz.	475 g	12 inches	30 cm
16 oz. (1 lb.)	500 g		
2 1b.	1 kg		

oven temperatures:

225°F	110°C	Gas ¼
250°F	120°C	Gas ½
275°F	140°C	Gas 1
300°F	150°C	Gas 2
325°F	160°C	Gas 3
350°F	180°C	Gas 4
375°F	190°C	Gas 5
400°F	200°C	Gas 6
425°F	220°C	Gas 7
450°F	230°C	Gas 8
475°F	240°C	Gas 9

index

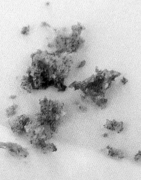